The Words of

MALCOLM X

Emmett Martin

PowerKiDS press.

Published in 2024 by The Rosen Publishing Group, Inc.
2544 Clinton Street, Buffalo, NY 14224

Portions of this work were originally authored by Sarah Machajewski and published as *Malcolm X in His Own Words*. All new material in this edition was authored by Emmett Martin.

Editor: Therese Shea
Book Design: Michael Flynn

Photo Credits: Cover https://commons.wikimedia.org/wiki/File:Malcolm-x_colorized_photo.jpg; (series background) merrymuuu/Shutterstock.com; (fact box) Miloje/Shutterstock.com; p. 5 https://en.wikipedia.org/wiki/File:Malcolm_X_NYWTS_2a.jpg; p. 7 ehrlif/Shutterstock.com; p. 9 https://commons.wikimedia.org/wiki/File:Malcolm_X_mugshot_1944.jpg; p. 11 (signature) https://commons.wikimedia.org/wiki/File:Malcolm_X_Signature.svg; p. 11 (Muhammad) https://commons.wikimedia.org/wiki/File:Elijah_Muhammad_NYWTS-2.jpg; p. 13 (bottom) Osugi/Shutterstock.com; p. 13 (top) https://commons.wikimedia.org/wiki/File:1965_FBI_monograph_on_Nation_of_Islam_-_Cult_newspaper.png; p. 15 Everett Collection Historical/Alamy Stock Photo; pp. 17, 19, 21 courtesy of the Library of Congress; p. 18 https://commons.wikimedia.org/wiki/File:John_F._Kennedy,_White_House_color_photo_portrait.jpg; p. 23 Pictorial Press Ltd/Alamy Stock Photo; p. 25 https://commons.wikimedia.org/wiki/File:MLK_and_Malcolm_X_USNWR_cropped.jpg; p. 27 Eczatasoy/Shutterstock.com.

Library of Congress Cataloging-in-Publication Data

Names: Martin, Emmett, author.
Title: The words of Malcolm X / Emmett Martin.
Description: New York : PowerKids Press, 2023. | Series: Historical
   perspectives: in their own words | Includes index.
Identifiers: LCCN 2022052379 (print) | LCCN 2022052380 (ebook) | ISBN
   9781642827071 (library binding) | ISBN 9781642827064 (paperback) | ISBN
   9781642827088 (ebook)
Subjects: LCSH: X, Malcolm, 1925-1965--Quotations--Juvenile literature. |
   Black Muslims--Biography--Juvenile literature. | African American civil
   rights workers--Biography--Juvenile literature.
Classification: LCC E185.97.L5 M378 2023 (print) | LCC E185.97.L5 (ebook)
   | DDC 320.54/6092 [B]--dc23/eng/20221214
LC record available at https://lccn.loc.gov/2022052379
LC ebook record available at https://lccn.loc.gov/2022052380

Manufactured in the United States of America

Some of the images in this book illustrate individuals who are models. The depictions do not imply actual situations or events.

CPSIA Compliance Information: Batch #CSPK24. For further information contact Rosen Publishing at 1-800-237-9932.

Find us on

CONTENTS

The 1960s in the United States are remembered as a time of counterculture. That means new and different ideas and values were introduced into larger American society. Many people were eager for social change, while others resisted it.

Some groups were pressing for equal rights under U.S. law. Black Americans were in the midst of a civil rights movement, demanding an end to **discrimination** based on race. In some areas, they were forced to attend separate schools, barred from voting, and experienced many other forms of injustice.

By the 1960s, slavery had been over for nearly 100 years in the United States, but change and acceptance for many Black Americans moved at too slow a pace. Malcolm X was one remarkable leader during this time who demanded an immediate end to **oppression**.

LOOKING BACK

Malcolm X's powerful words are still a source of inspiration to those fighting discrimination today.

Malcolm X was both **controversial** and respected in his own time. This book offers his speeches, letters, interviews, and other writings as a way to understand Malcolm's life and viewpoints. These are examples of primary sources, which are materials created by somebody who was present during a time in history. Primary sources give us an inside look at the person, and when and where they lived, through their own words rather than someone else's.

Other groups fighting for equality in the United States in the 1960s were women, Native Americans, and Mexican Americans.

Malcolm X was born with the name Malcolm Little on May 19, 1925, in Omaha, Nebraska. His parents, Earl and Louise, admired the teachings of Marcus Garvey, an **activist** who supported a separate Black society. Earl Little's own activism brought unwanted attention to the Little family. In 1929, the Littles' home was burned down. Then Earl was killed in an accident when Malcolm was six. Some, including Malcolm's mother, believed he had been murdered. Louise became mentally ill and was sent to a hospital, leaving the eight Little children to live with relatives or in foster care.

After dropping out of high school, Malcolm went to Boston, Massachusetts, to live with his sister Ella. He later said, "No physical move in my life has been more pivotal or **profound** in its **repercussions**."

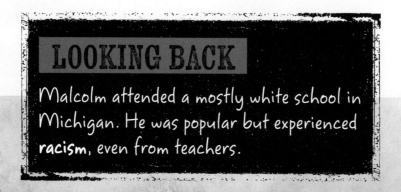

LOOKING BACK

Malcolm attended a mostly white school in Michigan. He was popular but experienced **racism**, even from teachers.

Dreams Dashed

Malcolm X was intelligent and did well in school, especially in his English and history classes. He was at the top of his class in junior high and was class president. He had dreams of becoming a lawyer. However, when he shared this idea with his favorite teacher, Mr. Ostrowski said it was "no realistic goal" for a Black man. Malcolm's success in school didn't seem to matter to him after that. He soon dropped out.

Lansing, Michigan

When Malcolm was still a baby, his family moved from Nebraska to Lansing, Michigan. Malcolm attended school there, but dropped out of high school.

In Boston, Malcolm worked a variety of jobs, including shining people's shoes. He became a gambler, drug dealer, and burglar. He joined a gang that committed crimes in Boston and New York City.

In 1946, Malcolm was arrested in Massachusetts and sentenced to 8 to 10 years in prison. This was a turning point in his life, but he said prison was the "greatest thing that ever happened" to him. It was there that he learned about the Nation of Islam.

Malcolm spent long hours studying the teachings of the Nation of Islam's leader, Elijah Muhammad. Malcolm told a magazine later that he was "nothing but another convict . . . [but the Nation's teachings] were able to reach into prison." The Nation of Islam offered him another life.

LOOKING BACK

The Nation of Islam is a religious organization that combines teachings of Islam and the Black nationalism movement. Nation members believe in Allah (Arabic for God) and follow traditional Islamic teachings, such as not using tobacco and alcohol.

Malcolm's parents had believed in Black nationalism. Based on ideas made popular by Marcus Garvey in the 1920s, the movement promoted pride in Black culture and history, the establishment of Black-owned businesses for economic independence, and a Black society separated from white society. In fact, Garvey had wanted to start a new nation in Africa. Similarly, Elijah Muhammad, the Nation of Islam leader, planned for a Black nation using land in Georgia, Alabama, and Mississippi.

This is Malcolm's mug shot, taken by the police after he was arrested for theft in 1944.

Followers of the Nation of Islam were encouraged to give up their last names because these names often came from white people who enslaved their ancestors. In a TV interview later, Malcolm explained, "During slavery, the same slavemaster who owned us put his last name on us to denote that we were his property." While some people took Muslim last names, others, like Malcolm, took the name "X."

When pressed by the TV host to tell him his father's last name, Malcolm stuck to his beliefs: "The last name of my forefathers was taken from them when they were brought to America and made slaves . . . We reject that [slave] name today and refuse it . . . I never acknowledge it whatsoever."

LOOKING BACK

Malcolm said, "For me, my 'X' replaced the white slavemaster name of 'Little' . . . imposed on my **paternal** forebearers."

Malcolm chose "X" as his last name because he would never know his African ancestors' names. The X represented the loss of identity experienced by enslaved people in the United States. Malcolm used X in all areas of his life, including when he married his wife, Betty, in 1958. She took the name Betty X. Later, they changed their last name again when Malcolm adopted another set of Islamic beliefs.

Malcolm X

While in prison, Malcolm regularly wrote to Elijah Muhammad, the leader of the Nation of Islam, who advised him to reject his past criminal life.

A NEW PURPOSE

Malcolm X was released from prison in 1952 and met with Elijah Muhammad in Chicago. Malcolm was inspired by the Nation of Islam leader. In a 1955 letter to his sister, Malcolm wrote that Muhammad's ideas "open your eyes to different things around you." The Nation of Islam gave Malcolm something to believe in. He thought it could do the same for others and set out to grow the Nation's membership.

Malcolm came to the Nation of Islam at a fitting time. The American civil rights movement was just beginning in the 1950s. Black Americans were organizing to combat the unfair treatment they experienced. Leaders with different **ideologies** started getting attention for their approaches to gaining equality. Soon, Malcolm would be included among them.

Elijah Muhammad

Elijah Muhammad was the leader of the Nation of Islam from the 1930s until his death in 1975. He was known for his extreme viewpoints, especially the way he talked about white people, sometimes calling them "blue-eyed devils." He also preached violence as a means of self-defense. Many people viewed him as racist. Some of Malcolm's early ideas that people admired or feared were from Elijah Muhammad.

LOOKING BACK

Malcolm helped establish the Nation of Islam's newspaper *Muhammad Speaks*. He asked members to sell these newspapers to spread their ideas and collect funds for the organization.

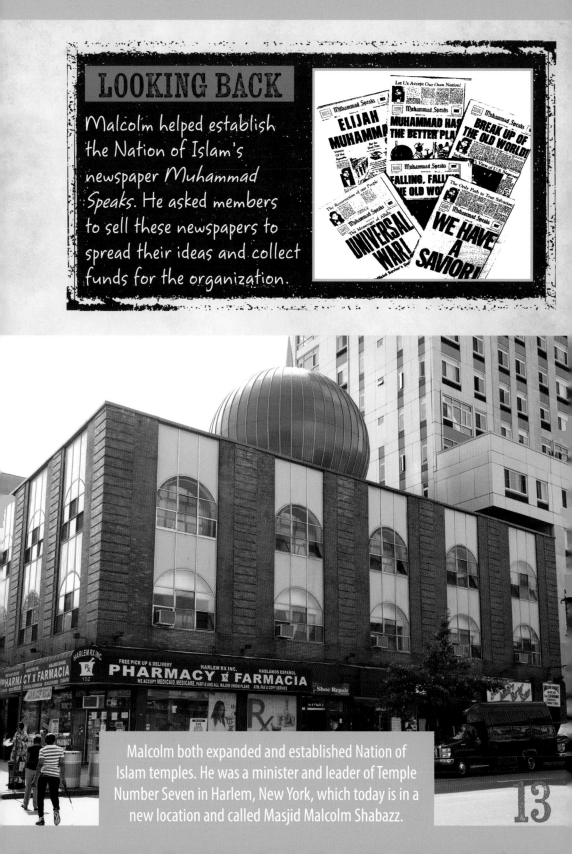

Malcolm both expanded and established Nation of Islam temples. He was a minister and leader of Temple Number Seven in Harlem, New York, which today is in a new location and called Masjid Malcolm Shabazz.

A 1959 television show called *The Hate That Hate Produced* featured interviews with several of the Nation of Islam's high-ranking officials, including Malcolm X. Malcolm was featured in the show saying that "by nature [the white man] is evil."

Viewers were shocked. The Nation of Islam came to be known as a hate group that was racist toward whites. Some members' extreme beliefs and angry speeches created a division between them and other civil rights activists of the time who preached nonviolence.

But some critics say that the producers made the Nation of Islam seem racist and scary. Malcolm agreed that, including the show's title, "every phrase was edited to increase the shock mood." Malcolm had become a nationally known figure because of it.

LOOKING BACK

One of the producers of *The Hate That Hate Produced* was Louis Lomax, the first Black American TV journalist.

Johnson Hinton

In 1957, a member of Malcolm X's Harlem temple–Johnson Hinton–was beaten by police. Malcolm called Nation of Islam members to take to the streets as he demanded that Hinton be given medical attention. Perhaps because of the large crowd, the police agreed. Hinton's ambulance was followed by Malcolm and a growing crowd of supporters. After Hinton received care, Malcolm dismissed the crowd of hundreds. A police officer remarked that no one should have that much power over others.

The Nation of Islam's membership rose after *The Hate That Hate Produced* aired. Above, Nation of Islam women attend a 1963 meeting.

AN EFFECTIVE LEADER

Malcolm's public speaking was effective. His commitment to the Nation of Islam and his way of communicating its ideas attracted many new members. The Nation of Islam would grow from 500 members in 1952 to over 30,000 by 1963. He was appointed the National Representative of the Nation of Islam in 1961, second only to Elijah Muhammad.

People paid attention to Malcolm because he expressed the anger and struggle experienced by Black Americans for decades—and he didn't apologize for it. "Just as the white man and every other person on this earth has God-given rights, natural rights, civil rights, any kind of right that you can think of when it comes to defending himself," he said, "Black people should have the right to defend ourselves also."

LOOKING BACK

Malcolm X said, "We don't hate anybody. We love our people so much they think we hate the ones who are inflicting injustice against them."

Many Black leaders of the civil rights movement, including Martin Luther King Jr., believed that their goal should be total **integration**. However, Malcolm X, Elijah Muhammad, and the Nation of Islam disagreed. They didn't want to live peacefully among the people who, they believed, had enslaved them and been racist toward them. "Complete separation is the only solution to the Black and white problem in this country," Malcolm maintained.

Many who heard Malcolm X speak said he was compelling. He tripled the membership of a Detroit temple in under a year.

Malcolm X's words crossed a line in late 1963, according to the Nation of Islam. In talking about the assassination, or killing, of President John F. Kennedy, Malcolm said, "I think this is a prime example of the devil's chickens coming back home to roost." He meant that Kennedy had failed to stop violence against Black people, so the violence came back and was committed against him.

People were shocked and offended by Malcolm's words. He further explained he meant the president's assassination was "a result of the climate of hate." Still, the Nation of Islam was embarrassed. Elijah Muhammad ordered Malcolm to stay silent for 90 days. Malcolm, who had had an increasing number of disagreements with Elijah Muhammad by that time, left the Nation of Islam in March 1964.

LOOKING BACK

President John F. Kennedy was assassinated on November 22, 1963, as he rode in a car through downtown Dallas, Texas.

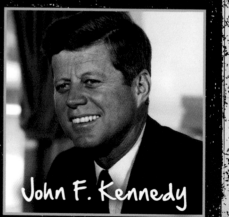

John F. Kennedy

JFK and Civil Rights

At first, President Kennedy had wanted to enforce civil rights laws already in place rather than pass new legislation. He appointed Black Americans to several government positions and supported the integration of schools. When the University of Alabama tried to keep Black students from enrolling, Kennedy sent the National Guard to force the school to integrate. After this, he announced he would send new civil rights legislation to Congress, which became the Civil Rights Act of 1964. Kennedy was assassinated before it passed.

Malcolm X disagreed with some of Elijah Muhammad's behaviors, which violated Nation of Islam teachings. Some said Muhammad saw Malcolm as a threat to his leadership too.

"BY ANY MEANS NECESSARY"

Malcolm X remained a person of interest to the American public even after he left the Nation of Islam. He used this as an opportunity to spread his message.

In one of his most famous speeches, in June 1964, he said, "We declare our right . . . to be a human being, to be respected as a human being, to be given the rights of a human being . . . which we intend to bring into existence by any means necessary." The "means" he talked about referred to everything—including violence. The phrase "by any means necessary" has become forever attached to Malcolm X's message. Malcolm made it clear that he didn't think **civil disobedience** was effective, especially for self-defense.

LOOKING BACK

Malcolm X's June 1964 speech came after his decision to form a group called the Organization of Afro-American Unity (OAAU). This group supported Pan-Africanism, a movement to strengthen bonds between all of African descent around the world.

The Right to Self-Defense

Malcolm X said, "The history of unpunished violence against our people clearly indicates that we must be prepared to defend ourselves or we will continue to be a defenseless people at the mercy of a ruthless and violent racist mob. . . . We assert that in those areas where the government is either unable or unwilling to protect the lives and property of our people, that our people are within our rights to protect themselves by whatever means necessary."

Malcolm considered the OAAU to be a human rights organization. It promoted Black control of every part of the Black community, including social programs.

LABELING MALCOLM

Malcolm X was accomplished at pointing out the deep-rooted racism of American society. But he himself was labeled as a racist. He addressed this and in a way that challenged white people to examine themselves. At a rally in New York in 1964, Malcolm declared, "They've always said that I'm antiwhite. I'm for anybody who's for freedom. I'm for anybody who's for justice. I'm for anybody who's for equality. . . . I'm not for anybody who tells Black people to be nonviolent while nobody is telling white people to be nonviolent."

Malcolm said he wasn't antiwhite: "I believe that there are some white people who might be sincere. But I think they should prove it." He wanted white Americans to fight for Black Americans' rights too.

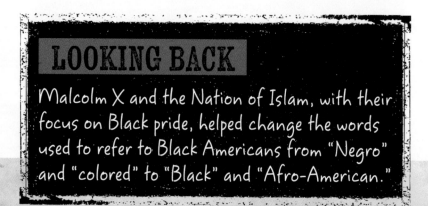

LOOKING BACK

Malcolm X and the Nation of Islam, with their focus on Black pride, helped change the words used to refer to Black Americans from "Negro" and "colored" to "Black" and "Afro-American."

People saw Malcolm as racist because he pointed the finger at white people for many problems Black Americans faced. He blamed white people for bringing enslaved Blacks to America and for having social, political, and economic systems that kept them unequal. But he said, "Now in speaking like this, it doesn't mean that we're anti-white, but it does mean we're anti-exploitation, we're anti-degradation, we're anti-oppression."

Because he had been the spokesperson for a group that was seen as racist and antiwhite, many people labeled Malcolm as those things too.

Malcolm X's ideas seemed strikingly different from those of another nationally famous leader of that time: Martin Luther King Jr. Malcolm was often asked for his opinions on King's ideology. He thought King's nonviolent approach was too weak in such a racist world.

King called on white and Black people to live peacefully together. He said, "Urging Negros to arm themselves and prepare to engage in violence . . . can reap nothing but grief."

But in Malcolm's view, King's goal was to get Black people "to forgive the people who have brutalized them for 400 years and . . . [make] them forget what those whites have done to them."

However, by 1964, after he left the Nation of Islam, Malcolm became more open to King's efforts for equality through the law.

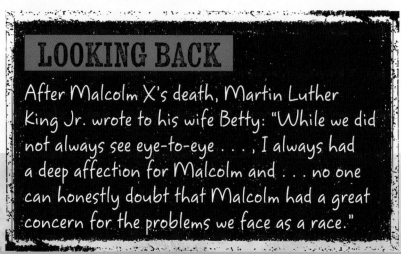

LOOKING BACK

After Malcolm X's death, Martin Luther King Jr. wrote to his wife Betty: "While we did not always see eye-to-eye . . . , I always had a deep affection for Malcolm and . . . no one can honestly doubt that Malcolm had a great concern for the problems we face as a race."

Reaching Out

Malcolm X said, "Dr. King wants the same thing I want — freedom!" In 1963, Malcolm wrote to King and other leaders inviting them to come together as a united front in Harlem: "It is a disgrace for Negro leaders to not be able to **submerge** our 'minor' differences in order to seek a common solution to a common problem." King didn't attend, however, and weeks later, Malcolm criticized King's March on Washington, calling it a "**farce** on Washington."

Martin Luther
King Jr.

Malcolm X and Martin Luther King Jr. met at a U.S. Senate discussion on the Civil Rights Act of 1964. They shook hands and spoke briefly. Malcolm said, "I'm throwing myself into the heart of the civil rights struggle."

Malcolm X still embraced his Muslim faith after he left the Nation of Islam. He founded Muslim Mosque, Inc., a new religious organization, in 1964. That same year, Malcolm traveled to Mecca, the holy Muslim city located in Saudi Arabia. He had a spiritual awakening there, embracing the Sunni branch of Islam. He changed his name to el-Hajj Malik el-Shabazz. He saw Muslims of all backgrounds, worshipping together. He met "blonde-haired, blue-eyed men I could call my brothers."

Malcolm returned to the United States rejecting the idea of separatism and with new hope for integration. His views of white people were changing too. Malcolm told a group of students in 1964 that "the most important thing we can learn to do today is think for ourselves."

LOOKING BACK

In Mecca, Malcolm X, now el-Hajj Malik el-Shabazz, wrote that he saw "pilgrims of all colors from all parts of this earth displaying a spirit of unity and brotherhood like I've never seen before."

In April 1964, Malcolm X gave a speech in Detroit now called "the Ballot or the Bullet" speech. While part of the Nation of Islam, Malcolm had been told not to get involved with politics or the mainstream civil rights movement, including voting registration. Now that he was no longer part of the Nation of Islam, he urged Black nationalists to get involved in politics: "The Black man in the Black community has to be re-educated into the science of politics."

Great Mosque of Mecca

"El –Hajj," the first part of Malcolm's new name, is a title given to someone who successfully completes a pilgrimage (*hajj*) to Mecca.

Malcolm X gained dangerous enemies after he left the Nation of Islam. He received death threats and attempts were made on his life. His home—with his family in it—was firebombed on February 14, 1965. All escaped unharmed. And still he said, "It isn't something that made me lose confidence in what I am doing."

On February 21, 1965, he was shot and killed as he was giving a speech in New York City. His wife Betty, pregnant with twins, and four of their children were there. Three Nation of Islam members were arrested.

Malcolm X—el-Hajj Malik el-Shabazz—died when he was 39 years old, as his views and goals for civil rights were still evolving. Today, his powerful words still challenge American society to fulfill its promise of equality.

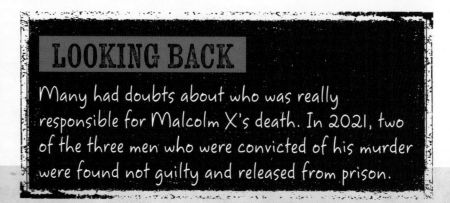

LOOKING BACK

Many had doubts about who was really responsible for Malcolm X's death. In 2021, two of the three men who were convicted of his murder were found not guilty and released from prison.

The Autobiography of Malcolm X

The Autobiography of Malcolm X was actually a biography, but the writer, Alex Haley, worked closely with Malcolm beginning in 1963. Malcolm didn't trust Haley at first, but the trust grew over time. Haley interviewed Malcolm many times, hearing his whole life story eventually, including his fallout with the Nation of Islam. Malcolm said, "I do not expect to live long enough to read this book in its finished form." Sadly, he was correct. People read the biography today to understand this complicated man better.

Timeline of Malcolm X's Life

1925 — Malcolm Little is born May 19 in Omaha, Nebraska.

1929 — The Little home burns in a fire, possibly begun by racists.

1931 — Malcolm's father is killed.

1941 — Malcolm moves to Boston, Massachusetts, to live with his sister.

1946 — He is arrested and imprisoned.

1947 — Malcolm is introduced to the Nation of Islam in prison.

1952 — Now Malcolm X, he is released from prison and moves to Detroit, Michigan.

1954 — Malcolm becomes minister of the Nation's Temple Number Seven in Harlem, New York.

1959 — *The Hate That Hate Produced* airs on television.

1963 — Malcolm is "silenced" by the Nation of Islam.

1964 — March — He leaves the Nation of Islam.

1964 — April — Malcolm journeys to Mecca and changes his name to el-Hajj Malik el-Shabazz.

1965 — He is assassinated on February 21 in New York City.

GLOSSARY

activist: A person who uses or supports strong actions to help make changes in politics or society.

civil disobedience: The breaking of a law as a form of nonviolent protest to force change.

controversial: Causing arguments.

discrimination: Unfairly treating people unequally because of their race or beliefs.

farce: Something seen as ridiculous.

ideology: A set of beliefs, values, and ideas that shape an individual.

integration: The act of opening a group, community, or place to all people.

oppression: The unjust use of power over another; treating people in a cruel or unfair way.

paternal: Having to do with the father's side of the family.

profound: Extending to great lengths.

racism: The belief that people of different races have different qualities and abilities and that some are superior or inferior.

repercussion: Something often bad that happens as a result of an action that affects people for a long time.

submerge: To put or sink below the surface of water.

FOR MORE INFORMATION

Books

Redmond, Jillian. *Malcolm X*. Broomall, PA: Mason Crest, 2019.

Vietze, Andrew. *The Life and Death of Malcolm X*. New York, NY: Rosen YA, 2018.

Wilkins, Ebony. *Malcolm X: Get to Know the Civil Rights Activist*. North Mankato, MN: Capstone Press, 2020.

Websites

Malcolm X Through the Years
abcnews.go.com/US/photos/malcolm-years-29114886/image-29115811
Read about events in Malcolm's life, paired with photographs.

Speeches and Interviews
ccnmtl.columbia.edu/projects/mmt/mxp/speeches/index.html
Read and listen to Malcolm X's speeches on this Columbia University site.

INDEX